Penelope Returning

Penelope Returning

Collected Poems

Susan Ford Wiltshire

Penelope Returning

Copyright © 2021 by Susan Ford Wiltshire

All rights reserved. No part of this book may be reproduced in any way without the expressed, written consent of the publisher.

"For John," "Mrs. Wilson," and "Easter Poem II" first appeared in *Seasons of Grief and Grace* (Vanderbilt University Press, 1994).

"Mentor," "Grafted" (as "Evolution"), and "Molly Todd at Ninety" (as "Molly") were originally published in *Athena's Disguises* (Westminster John Knox Press, 1998).

"Molly Todd at Ninety" (as "Molly") also appeared in the *Tennessean*, March 24, 1996, 5D.

"Evolutionary Artist" appeared in *number: an independent journal of the visual arts #38* (Summer, 2000) 26.

"Sounds of a Windmill" (as "Translation"), "Planting Iris," "My Son" (as "Meo Filio Aetat 1"), "Harvest in the Barn," "Scissored," "How Fledglings Leave the Nest" (as "Vigil"), "Alchemy," "Mrs. Wilson," "For John," "Split Decision," "Easter Poem II," "Reverse Samaritan," "Hieroglyph," "Abecedarium," "Positive," "Sibling Song," "First Day Out on a Long Journey," "No Free Verse," "Tethered," "Second Harvest," "Formation," "St. Gregory's Hole," "Janissary / Harem," "Revised" (as "Returning, Revised"), "Evolutionary Artist," "Mentor," "Grafted" (as "Evolution"), "Molly Todd at Ninety" (as "Molly"), "After Five Years" (as "Lustrum"), "Capital Punishment" (as "Relent"), "Corpus Christi," "Lines upon Losing a Journal," "Haiku," and "Penelope Returning" were previously published in *Windmills and Bridges* (Eakin Press, 2002).

"First Day Out on a Long Journey," "Revised" (as "Returning, Revised"), "No Free Verse," "Sex and the Barnyard," "My Son" (as "Meo Filio Aetat 1"), "Scissored" (as "Launched"), "Mentor," "You Can't Marry Everyone You Love," "Lines upon Losing a Journal," and "To Vergil, His Birthday" appeared in *The Long View* (Cordelia Hollis Publishing, 2015).

ISBN: 978-0-578-33270-3

Cordelia Hollis Publishing
54 George Harvey Ln.
McEwen, TN 37101

*to Nancy Felson
and sixty years of friendship*

Penelope Returning

Seeds
Positive 2
The Secret 3
Reverse Samaritan 4
Mentor 5
Alchemy 6
Hieroglyph 7
Abecedarium 8

Hearth
Planting Iris 10
My Son 12
Harvest in the Barn 13
Scissored 15

Brother
For John 18
Split Decision 19
Mrs. Wilson 20
Easter Poem II 22
After Five Years 24
Sibling Song 26

Companions
You Can't Marry Everyone You Love 30
Grafted 31
Evolutionary Artist 32
Molly Todd at Ninety 33

Of One Whose Art Washed Away in a Flood
After Her Death 36
Love Poem for a Couple in Their Eighties 37
Haiku 38

Farming
Sex and the Barnyard 40
How Fledglings Leave the Nest 42
Sounds of a Windmill 45

Legacies
Cincinnatus Saves Rome and Goes Home 47
Corpus Christi 48
Capital Punishment 49
Mary at Forty-Eight 50
To Vergil, His Birthday 52

Elsewhere
First Day Out on a Long Journey 56
Lines upon Losing a Journal 57
No Free Verse 62
St. Gregory's Hole 63
Janissary / Harem 64
Tethered 65
Formation 66
Second Harvest 67
Revised 69
Penelope Returning 70

Without the arts, we would be poor creatures indeed, slumping sullenly from sleep to food to work to food and back to sleep again. The arts—painting, sculpture, music, dance, theater, the written and spoken word in all its forms—not only enhance life, they are life. They add flesh to the curves and colors and leaps of spirit that make us truly human.

Seeds

Positive

Think positive, chirped the worker
at the gym as I left for the good day
I was instructed also to have.

How, I thought, in her innocence
could she presume to fit the same advice
to every stranger she salutes?

At the moment I passed her by
I was plumbing the murk, dead set
on making sense of some unopinioned dark.

For an instant I was enticed to hoist
my sail wide and white as a smile,
set to scud breezily into the day.

But, being peculiarly curious,
I held instead to the work of discerning
what is below the surface I traverse

so when I arrive at the other side
I'll know the whole of where I've been,
the reefs as well as the gleamy sea.

The Secret

Secretum est
Audire disastram
Sperare triumpham
Et describere formas incarnationis

The secret is
To dare disaster
Hope for triumph
And describe the forms of the Incarnation

Reverse Samaritan

On rare roads
the most generous act
possible toward a person
who causes hurt by habit
is to pass kindly by,
depositing at the inn
not the wounded wounder
but the tiresome tedium
of one's own righteousness.

Mentor

You will not know
the moment when
instead of seeking
you are sought.
And if you are,
you will not notice
because you yourself
will still be seeking,
seeing and sometimes
choosing the brambled
byways where lies
a lonely cistern,
cenotaph to souls
once lively there,
or strange new friend,
or poem that will
not let you go.

Maybe, only once or more
as you lean into a curve,
you will catch at the
periphery of your vision
a younger one watching you,
what it is you are looking for.

Alchemy

tene plumbum, aurum sequeter
Hold on to the lead, the gold will follow

Newton studied alchemy for years
because he believed God acts
in every element of the universe
so even lead can change to gold.

Four centuries later, Vladimir Haensel
added platinum to fossil fuel.
All was gain: higher octane without the lead,
raw materials for plastics remained.

On a day he was honored,
Haensel spoke of the power of catalysis,
how bodies loosen, break down, reform,
old always turning into new.

Listening rapt, she thought of writers:
If they follow faithfully enough
the practice of pencil upon the page,
their lead too may turn to gold.

Hieroglyph

Burdened by a list of duties
she dreaded doing,
she decided instead
to translate tasks
into hieroglyphs,
summoning into pictures
the meanings they contained.

These depictions
formed upon her page:
The privilege of stewardship;
Music for stirring the day;
Time with a wise ally;
Sharing a book that mattered;
Making something new.

This holy script transformed
the dun of duty
into the compass of love.

Abecedarium

Avoid abstractions
Be creative
Care calmly
Dare defeat
Enjoy children
Fear not at all
Get up early
Hold on
Invest in the impossible
Judge sparingly
Know solitude
Love laughter
Make big mistakes only once
Need knowingly
Organize
Practice politics
Quit worrying
Risk writing
Sin bravely
Trust God more bravely
Understand
Venture far
Walk or run
XV miles every week, and let
Youth be less
Zealous than age.

Hearth

Planting Iris

I loved iris for years before I planted any,
then a hundred over a week or more
one September when I was fifty-five.

As I dug I puzzled over where I got it from,
why it was iris I wanted to plant
more than any other thing I might have done,

could think of no one in my family
who cared for flowers anyway
except one great-grandmother
who died the day that I turned five.

When the work was done I called my mother,
told her of the planting. She said
Not a spring went by that your father
did not say he wished he had
planted iris the fall before.

So then I knew, one tiny piece I had
not known, never heard him say it,
but knew it true in the marrow of my bone.

Bone? Is the love of iris buried deep
there too in some baffling dance
of those gyring spirals of DNA?

If I could know only one lettered
sequence of the four nucleotides
of one gene of one chromosome
of those twenty-three resolute pairs
that cast me upon the shore
as who I thought I only was,

what more might I yet learn
of the abyss that is the father
I deigned to think I knew
but did not know loved iris?

My Son
Age 1

after Catullus

Ludis ut passer volitans circum nunc
gremium meum, fortiter, libenter.
Cum tandem te emittere erit necesse,
tum precor ut sim, similis te, fili,
  libera et fortis.

You play now like a sparrow
flying around my breast, bravely, freely.
When at last it will be necessary to let you go,
I pray that I may be like you, child,
  Free and brave.

Harvest in the Barn

Come end of June
the harvest, if there is one,
is in the barn.

And so it was
when our dear fledgling
returned to roost
before her next flight out.

We passed our days in such delight
it could have broke my heart
had not all been so gentle
and so right.

Still I,
who know of hail and drought,
doubted whether I deserved
to have my harvest in the barn
at all, and all the more
when I surveyed my neighbors' fields
and saw their crops
at risk of being lost
as ours so nearly was.

Then I recalled that harvests
are not for barns
but for the hungry.
Barns are only for safekeeping
for the passing through.

Then I knew
the answer to my doubt,
and my brief flirt with guilt
gave way to summer
savored to the hilt.

Scissored

On her final college holiday
our daughter, latter-born of two,
Prepared furiously through the night
for her first job interview.

I circled in her radius.
Why are you staying up? she asked.
You're supporting me, aren't you?
Of course, I said. I was, of course.

At the airport door she walked straight
through without a backward glance.
We watched her disappear into the crowd,
turned to one another in wonderment.

I felt scissored, as surely as
our firstborn's start at kindergarten,
when I wandered blindly by the office to see
if they had any counseling for me.

This departure was the final one.
The last one's leaving meant
that both had left forever
the safe familiar of our world.

For them this is continuum, their worlds
circling larger while still including ours.
For me, it was completion, a gate
I traversed at the far end of a field

I tended for over twenty years—
breaking, tilling, planting, cultivating,
weeding, protecting, fending off
the terrifying pass of storms.

What those dear two do not know is that
I too begin new voyages to far lands
of mind and spirit. Only a simulacrum mom
waits hopefully home by the phone.

I pause at the gate, waft a prayer
of gratitude for the harvested field behind,
take measure of the trackless plain ahead,
and slowly start the crossing.

Brother

For John

> Even in our sleep, pain we cannot
> forget falls
> drop by drop upon the heart, until, in our
> despair, against our will, comes
> wisdom through the awful grace of the gods.
> —Aeschylus

Leaving, I grieve
the limits of love,
that I cannot build a bulwark against
the sliding places of your life.

No. I am wrong.
To wish that
is to deny your power
to do it for yourself
or to presume that I could know
the landscape of your need.

Instead, I reach out like a girder
over the traffic of our lives
to connect with you,
tighten the bolts,
and build together a brace sufficient against
any wind.

Split Decision

There is no shield in the Desert Storm
for that child first time out of Kentucky.

The only thing shrinking about our friend's
lymphoma is the hopes of her friends.

The world's sorrows eclipse mine,
my brother said as he called to tell me his,

citing the boys and girls in the desert
and the young mother's cancer,

but grieving the loss
of a place to love and to die.

Comparing sorrows commits violence
against the sorrowing, I know,

but he is my near brother, so
I, only sister, will reach

out to share the sorrows of others,
in to share his.

Mrs. Wilson

"You want to be immortal?"
asked the preacher at Easter.
"Love somebody."

Mrs. Wilson, having known exclusion,
knew to take in the exiled.
So she took care of "her boys"
in the rebirthplace of democracy,
the nation's capital,
in the zip code that meant no life insurance,
heinous mark of Cain.

She was mother to orphans
whose own had disowned them—
caring, cleaning, loving,
sharing the beloved spaniel Mrs. B.

Best of all, she was hospitality.
With her they did not have to
hide the dailiness
of their lives together.

They loved her back before they died.
One did more:
He was her friend.
He went to her home in the projects,
along the train line to Philadelphia
where she had raised her own children well.
Having no time or money,
he gave her both
on a deep winter day.

She died at Easter.
Some fine Easter he would too.
No matter.
They are forever.

Easter Poem II

I promised you
we would build a girder
across our lives
sufficient against any wind.

But how could I know then
that you would become the wind?
Powerful even when still,
moved by forces you may know now,
not the callow fripperies
of some eddying breeze
but the inexorable tide
of the Panhandle sky.

Or are you altogether gone
who always loved to wander?
Did you follow the sound
of the outward bound
one last time,
a mariner off to the stars?

But if you are altogether gone,
why am I sometimes bent to the ground,
hapless as wheat against
a blue Texas norther?

Why do I sometimes howl at the moon
like a coyote in the scant hiatus of
dead calm before dusk?
Why, in these still hollows of Tennessee,
have I come to feel most at home

when a strong wind blows?

Why, at last, in my sad loss,
against my will, do I begin to sense,
sometimes, almost as a blessing,
the wind at my back?

After Five Years

His fifth Christmas and birthday
snapped shut like a spring-hinged trap
on a wide-eyed creature terrified
at her sudden incapacity.

Other anniversaries she had dreaded,
memorialized, raged against, smiled
a tear upon. The waves were settling.
Why was this December different?

The Romans knew the power of the lustrum,
a five-year span of measure so laden
they made for it a rite of purification
so life could right itself again.

I do not know the ways or reason
of their ministrations, only that I
flailed my loss this year wrought
tightly as a wounded animal caught.

How I saw "Angels in America," was flung
back to the time before the choice and chore
of living long instead of dying well,
could imagine nothing but your perfect death.

How our last journey took me away from
other loves, those closest that I chose,
husband first, and children, friends
who patiently waited through my grief.

How your last beloved Christmas Eve
I overcompensated, stayed with them
at the Cathedral service instead of being
home with you. What must you have thought?

How I lost another brother the day
that I lost you, no longer trying
to make right what no one could
but we two had long committed to.

Now I have said the hard things.
Maybe it takes five years to say them,
maybe that is why this anniversary is so raw
I only now can cauterize the edges of recall.

Sibling Song

Our oldest story holds Cain against Abel.
Being brother or sister
to sister or brother is laden with danger.

Joseph's brothers could not bear their father's
favor toward his lastborn fair, so sold him
into slavery for his Lakers coat.

Hector's fool of a brother caused much trouble for Troy
by choosing Aphrodite who beguiled him with
promises of another man's wife

if he would judge her fairest of her female kin
who themselves were competing for the
age-old prize of prettiest.

Wolf-suckled Romulus slew his twin for the rule
      of Rome.
The warring brothers of Thebes killed each other
in one sally of spears at the walls of home.

Are we all chained to Cain in this script with no sense?
If God made the choice that caused Cain's despite,
why did innocent Abel die?

Would siblings compete with no prizes to gain?
Are they so fearful of offending a father
they inflict their rage on each other?

* * * * * *

It is not always so, does not have to be.
Two at least were linked in soul from
the moment he arrived, then she—

sooner, perhaps, if their two hearts beat out
a frail tattoo in unison in their cocoon's
dark swelling sea.

She said the union between them was different
in kind from their relations
with the other six:

If one were hungry or hurt, the other knew.
They never were on opposite sides.
They were a team, she said.

Each night they fixed their minds upon eternity
(the pact between them no other guessed),
each vying to bid the last goodnight.

In their family of scientists, she heard him ask:
Does God sit down to lunch each day?
Does God love chimney sweeps?

When she chose a mate, he embraced him too,
became his friend, helped both escape
when lawless bans imperiled them.

He made his own way, theologian, man for others, found
another who shared his great faith,
cornflowers free by the fields.

At the end he yet said yes to life, tutored from the womb
by the sister who survived him half a century,
whole and fine—wife, mother, friend—

but for all her days in unanticipated moments felt
half her heart constrict with missing him
like an amputated limb.

---

*in memory of Dietrich Bonhoeffer, February 4, 1906-April 9, 1945,
and Sabine Bonhoeffer Leibholz, February 4, 1906-July 7, 1999

Companions

You Can't Marry Everyone You Love

You are
The song I will not sing
The ring I will not wear
The dare I will not choose
The music I won't know
The poem I will not write
The night I will not dream
The stream I will not cross.
So what remains from all this loss?

You are
The polished dance floor where I glide
The morning star that seems a guide
The shade you make I often rest in
The burnished map of where I've been.

This love more lasting than surprise,
This love that's kind and fair and wise.

Grafted

The oak is in the acorn, they say of trees,
but not of me, whose limbs
assume new lineaments
in the company of friends.

Evolutionary Artist

for Sylvia Hyman

Porcelain is the purest clay, kaolin decomposed
where it lay, gathering no alloy along the way,
fine as old wine, pliant, elegant—like her.

No dilettante, she knew she was an artist from
the age of eight, claimed her calling full-time
when time allowed, mentor to many then and now.

She traveled, taught, could not conceive a day
when the magic of her fingers would resist
rolling the tiny beads she was famous for.

After arthritis, she smiled, invented new ways
of rolling clay, forming scrolls compelling as Qumran,
stacked in piles, gathered in baskets real as gardens.

Over eighty now, her racing hands cannot keep pace
with her laughing imagination, her evolving art,
curious as chromosomes, surprising as genes.

Molly Todd at Ninety

You lie in purple circled with pearls,
nearly empty of the ninety years you've earned.
Reaching among stringless beads of memory
for the names of your children,
you nevertheless greet guests
with a kindness that would be courtly
except for your accustomed modesty.

It is a modesty surely practiced,
for you had much to be modest for:
Sturdy stander-by of those who dared
to take forbidden seats where
anyone of lighter hue could eat;
Persistent rouser-up of those
who would not stand for anything;
Loved by many, feared by some
because you were afraid of none.

A visitor recalls a protest you directed
against one more fool reactor at Oak Ridge
twenty years ago when you were young.

"Yes," you say, "I seem to remember that.
We won, didn't we?" (It was a question.)
We did. And it was you who made it fun.

(No size-eight social matron she,
with rounded shoes and pointed pedigree,
coiffed and clad in good gray wool,
intently bent on doing good.

In her was quality far less tame,
the inborn power of some handsome beast
guarding the borders of the plain
with watchful eye and perfect ease.)

When was that splice of time for you—
were you thirty-seven? fifty-two?—
when for a moment all was bright:
children strong, parents well,
braced around by thriving kin,
and you were full of will and mind
to tackle wrong of every kind?·

Were you wise enough in those fleet days
to savor color when you passed it by,
smiling with knowledge it would not last
and still was good and was a gift?

Surely you were then as you are now,
calmly responding when someone asks
if you are frustrated by all
that is fugitive from your recall.
"No," you say simply. "We all forget."

You continue:
"I sleep a great deal.
Fortunately I sleep easily.
I wake up, note the time,
then fall asleep again."

But later you add:
"Now there is nothing
I can give to anyone.
That is what I'm sorry for."

No.
Because you are here
in shape and form and name,
you summon stories from your guests
that offer recall to yourself.
That pleases you, you say.

What you do not see with your fine eyes
(the morning paper lies nearby)
is the good you do the storytellers,
whose best is leavened by what they tell.

That is the gift you give and will
until the moment you depart
(sooner than the hours feel
though not as soon as you may wish}.

And then?
Then you will continue on
in memory authentic
as the pearls you wear.

---

* This poem is dedicated to Federal Judge Cissy Daughtrey, one of whose opinions led to the 2015 Supreme Court ruling on marriage equality.

Of One Whose Art Washed Away in a Flood After Her Death

> Art washes away the dust of everyday life.
> —Picasso

The water rose, rose again,
Faster and further than thought,
and washed away all her art.

But in our grief
we fail to see that she herself
does not repent the loss.

The moment she added that
last bold stroke to canvas,
she stepped back, looked,

smiled, nodded, turned away
and let it go, knowing at last
how good an artist she was.

She, who stared down loss
all her life, had washed away at last
the dust of doubt about her art.

Love Poem for a Couple in Their Eighties

(long after Catullus 5)

Let us live, my dear, and let us love—
And let us count the sneers of jealous scolds
As worth less than a cent.

The sun is able to set and rise again,
But once our brief light goes out
It won't be coming back.

So give me a thousand kisses,
Then a hundred,
Then a thousand
Then a hundred more.

And when we've kissed
As much as we could
We'll pretend we didn't,
And all those souls who envy us
Won't know how much they should.

Haiku

Lovers first, they bowed
and began the long slow dance
of friends to the last.

Farming

Sex and the Barnyard

(For city folk who might not know)

The bovine genders divide easily in half
A cow is a heifer who's had her first calf.
A bull is a male who breeds and butts.
A steer is a bull who's lost his nuts.

The equine terms are not willy-nilly:
A mare is a female, born as a filly
until she engages in sexual melding
with any fine stallion but never a gelding.

A horse and a donkey breed to make mules,
but this noble race endures different rules.
The mom is a mare horse, the daddy's a jack
but though sex is what makes them, they can't do it back.

And now for the porcines, whence comes the bacon
and sausage you really should see in the making,
the sows are the mamas of every small piglet,
the boars are those who strut by and jiggle it.

As for the goats, who do well where it's hilly,
the she is a nannie, the he is a billy.
And as for the sheep and the making of lambs
the ewes are those who consort with the rams.

I see I've passed over the wethers and shoats.
You'll need to know both if you're worth your oats.
Shoats are weaned pigs facing lives of hard knocks,
wethers are rams who've been docked in the crotch.

Thus comes the end of this rustical ditty
meant to take sex right out of the city
and back to the barnyard, a simpler land,
where coupling is casual and wholly unplanned.

How Fledglings Leave the Nest

I wanted to know
how baby birds leave the nest.
Do they fall first,
then fly from the ground?

Are they pushed out by their mother?
Do all fly at once?
What time of day do they leave?
How do they know when to go?

(If you have seen how this happens,
skip over this poem and go to the next.)

* * * 🕊 * * *

Small black birds like swallows
build nests on our porch every season.
Each year I count eggs, know when they hatch,
hope always to catch them ready to fly.

Always before I found only their leavings.
This year four young were still in the nest
and I had long summer days to invest.

Here's what I saw in my vigil:

Birds sleep at night as we do,
so I watched only by day.
Mothers feed themselves first,
I noted intently. Nestling breakfast
begins about quarter to six. Mouths gape.

At first that was all the babes could do,
chirp and gape. Then they started
flexing their wings in the nest,
circling their tails over the side.

That was their first independence,
going to the bathroom alone.
(I should have known.)
If the mother was swooping by at the time,
she caught the poop neatly and took it away.

Sometimes she caught a piece in midair.
She did not seem to care what fell below,
but the nest itself she always kept clean.
This caretaking filled all her day.

For two days I watched, never bored.
Sometimes the fledglings huddled primly
like penguins. Mostly they chittered,
especially as mother approached with a bite.

More and more they seemed to be practicing:
Sometimes they perched on nestside
facing in, holding on for dear life, whirring
their wings in a blur fast as hummingbirds.
What caused them to know how to go?
No nestlings nearby cajoled them
to come out and play, taunting them
like teenagers to flee from their home.

Finally, on the third afternoon,
one flew out on his own, flapped wildly
toward the opposite wall, hit the ceiling,
returned to the ledge alongside the nest.

Three beaks pivot toward him. Mother
feeds him outside of the nest. A second
flutters out for a visit, then retreats.
Mother feeds the three still in the nest.

Sometimes she chooses, sometimes she
feeds the first one who begs.
Suddenly all goes quiet. Are they resting?
Is the cat out? Is other danger nearby?

Then it happened: Three of them flew away
almost at once, bounced off the low ceiling,
got their bearings, whirled to a nearby tree.

One stayed behind, seemingly without dismay.
After a while he looked around,
hopped onto the edge of the nest,
sailed off, hit the ceiling,
swooped under the roof and onto a tree.

This I saw.
I have heard this:
fledglings their first night out
of the nest huddle together
on a branch for warmth.

I hope it is true.

Sounds of a Windmill

At night the sounds of a windmill
sidle up as company against
the ceaseless assail
of the wind:

kindly clunks, not quite melodic,
of galvanized sheet metal fans
and tail fin catching the wind
as they bend;

sturdy thumps every twenty seconds or so
as check balls plunk into reverse
to lift life four hundred feet
to our need.

Legacies

Cincinnatus Saves Rome and Goes Home

We should not have won our Revolution
We should not have won our Constitution.
Both required the work of everyone
But depended on the character of one.

The artists saw it first.*

King George III asked American-born Benjamin West
"What will Washington do next? Will he be King
or Chief of the Army?" West smiled in reply,
"His only desire is to go home to Mount Vernon."

Charles Willson Peale was commissioned
To paint a portrait of the hero Cincinnatus
for a celebration of America' new nation.
The old Roman closely resembled George Washington.

Jean-Antoine Houdon came to Mount Vernon
To create Washington's likeness from life.
His sculpture depicts the farmer back home,
Plow at his feet, walking stick in his hand.

Constantino Brumidi's first commission
for the new Capitol walls depicted
Cincinattus choosing between duty and plow.
How should public servants bow out? That's how.

---

* Benjamin West   1738-1820
  Charles Willson Peale   1741-1827
  Jean-Antoine Houdon 1741-1828
  Constantino Brumidi   1805-1880

Corpus Christi

A town in Texas,
a gathering of the faithful,
the body of Christ, a McNally play.

My good brother and I
grew up in the wings
of all those worlds

played out on the stage that day
thirty-five years after another
hate crime in a Dallas street.

Never before had I entered a theater
through metal detectors and guards
eyeing faces contorted with rage.

All right, you say, let's talk about it:
What if Jesus wasn't gay?
That's fine. It's only that

he could have been, or different skin,
or woman, if Incarnation means
God came out as one of us.

The dissenters' greatest wrath,
if only they had had the wit
to dare come in and see the play,

would have been how happy were
the faces of those who lived within
His company that day.

Capital Punishment

Lent is one long
Saturday before
Easter, dumb denial
of the gruesome death
by legal torture
of the day before.

How on that one day
at least could any
Christian rise in
righteous vindication
of the state's right still
to kill that way?

Mary at Forty-Eight

Quick, how old was Mary, the mother of Jesus?
In paintings and sculptures does she ever have wrinkles?
Why in Michelangelo's Pieta does she look younger
than the dead son she is cradling?

If Mary was, say, fifteen when Jesus was born,
she would have been forty-eight when he died.
John 19:25 says Mary was standing by
the cross of her son as he died.

Grammar matters. The Greek verb says
the women had gathered and were standing by.
Mary kept on standing by.
Why did she not faint or flinch or stay away?

    At forty-eight, Mary had seen much in her lifetime
    and had pondered it all in her heart.

She had seen trust broken and children violated.
She had seen people cheat and bully the weak.
She resented Roman hostility to her beliefs
and having to live in an occupied land.

She had survived flood and drought,
which meant no crops and less food.
She had felt anger at the fool's triumph
and the best laborer dead and all the sheaves to bind.*

Mary knew that horrible things happen
but they are never the last things.
She was heartbroken when her son died,
but she was not confounded.

---

* With appreciation to W.B. Yeats.

To Vergil, His Birthday

I dreamed of you once—
a tall man, dark, countrified,
dressed in old black suit and fedora,
standing silent against a wall.

Months later I realized it was you
I followed that day at the airport,
abandoning toys at the baggage claim,
dodging bullies bent on stopping me.

You passed the gate up to the plane,
I squeezed through just in time,
knowing I would follow you—
where did not matter.

You were more ambitious than your peers
but not as most Romans were ambitious.
You, who knew power,
stayed away from Rome.

You dared to compose a story
better than Homer's, public and private.
You wrote it both ways,
as a Libra would.

Your few close friends survived:
Varius, Tucca, but most of all Horace.
I hope he loved you back.
It took you both to write what each one wrote.

You averaged three lines a day.
Were there days you did not work at all?
Were you ever depressed, hopeless?
Most of all, my ally, I ask this:

How was it when you finished?
Why did you beg others to burn it?
Was it something in the poem
or in you that was not right?

Did you really wonder how the wrath
in celestial minds could be so great?
I think you knew it is in our minds
where that wrath is.

Dear Vergil, when you died at fifty-one,
what was left for you to do?
After Homer you had matched the best,
told the hardest stories closest to the bone.

Could I be living on for you,
a dozen shores and more away,
unwilling to annul public,
unable to abjure private,

wondering ever how to read
the past through palimpsests,
like you a farmer, steward of heritage,
seeking all ways to make the old new?

Your poem ends with *umbras*.
Once I found that sad. No longer.
Now I like shadows. They are companions—
bread for the journey.

Shadows change, lengthen, contract,
fade and come again,
like kindness or a friend.
What you see depends on where you stand.

Elsewhere

First Day Out on a Long Journey

Leaning forward alone
up the swaying gangway of a strange ship
with new mates or old made odd
in the absence of all familiar,

no hooks for hanging expectation on,
a failure of nerve descends.
Back-home anticipations, so etched and eager,
clinging to doorposts like a joyless child

in time are shaken away like water from a spaniel
pointing with determination
toward a horizon as unmarked
and receding as the sea.

Finally she laughs at all that is left behind,
turns to stride into the unknown
that will become familiar when tamed
by habit and time and delight.

Lines upon Losing a Journal

> Losing a passport is an inconvenience
> Losing a journal is a disaster
> —Robert Martins

Hurrying to leave the train at Pisa
I left behind the record of the weeks before
and grieved that with the record
all was lost.

Once I knew the small bound book was gone for good
after all efforts to find it failed, I worried
the absence like a child the space left by a
new-pulled tooth.

The dailiness, I knew, could be reconstructed according
    to the need.
The names alone of places stayed could serve
as suns governing by their gravity whole
circuits of stories:

Astoria Nomikos Galini Kalypso Olympic Victoria
Suisse Adua Bartoli Consoli di Mare Milano San Marco—
each a small lifetime compressed into syllables,
diamonds from coal.

But what of the dreams that graced each day with
color, raiment, shape—those thoughts that flocked
unbidden, metamorphosing slowly into meaning
as I watched?

How do I salvage those while the wind blows rain
hard against my pane in Castiglioncello
where finally I landed after a bleak diversion
through unlovely Livorno?

* * * * * *

How it felt to circle the Martinengo Bastion of old
Iraklion where Kazantzakis lies beneath a stone
      that reads
"I hope for nothing, I fear nothing, I am free" but
bears no name.

How later in that dear narrow room in Rome
at 26 Piazza di Spagna, I wondered if Nikos knew what
clear-eyed Keats demanded, that a poet's name be writ
in water only.

How at that same door in '44 the soldier-poet of the
Second War, the one descended from Archilochus,
knocked to announce "I am a student" and rejoiced to
surrender to poetry.

How my room at the Nomikos Villa was a trapezoid
wedged into the core of the volcano, widening toward
the caldera of Santorini like a birth canal from the
center of earth.

How I felt when I saw Hermes holding the smiling child
at Olympia, both of them coaxed (at what cost?)
out of marble from the mines at Paros I had visited only
a day before.

How I came to see that the corridor from the high plains
of Texas to just south of Taos, where the air is composed
of the same humors as I am—old Epicurus believed
souls are matter—

skips like a stone over an ocean and several seas to
the flat high-skied Aegean where I feel the same primeval
oneness that Parmenides said once was true of
all of us.

How Rome became at once so much more like home
and so much more remote from all my grasp
that I embraced her as I might
a furtive lover

whom I must flee before first light, before
first pealing of the bells all round
so not to be caught lying
with a stranger.

How Michelangelo's Last Judgment says no one thing
but how his Expulsion from the Garden does:
that the very knowledge that makes us human will also
break our hearts.

How I felt an uncontestable shifting of the poles from
Righting Wrong to Writing Plain, and how I wondered
which of these—or is it friends?—will matter most when
all is done.

How there were moments en route when I felt as if
    I were
living the story I'm writing as surely as a quilter
piecing the leftover fragments of multiple
lives into art.

How dearly I seek to convey all those characters lurking
in my brain like Michelangelo's prisoners
into a braille writ clear enough for all the
world to see.

How Florence in June at least has imploded
with so vast a horde of earnest weary tourists
that the scholars, painters, master builders
of all her art

would scatter in panic if they knew,
leaving only the Medici capitalists
to make from all the consumers
one last florin.

How Michelangelo knew what Vergil knew, what so
        few do,
that it is possible, but only by the finest hew,
to tell the truth and please
the patron too.

How Brunelleschi's double dome is a metaphor
not for a city only but for life, the one enclosing
the vast unknown within, the other, that without,
and how we,

like his laborers, traverse the narrow catwalks between
the two, their curves dizzying us always bending over,
with nothing at a distance we can see
to steady us,

until, pausing in the endless work to steal
a bite or kiss, we catch through tiny windows
a shining glimpse of the vast round plate below or
azure bowl above

and know then that the work is good, even if
we must soon descend the tiny curl of steps down
toward the door that exits to or from the world in
one direction only.

How I asked myself then if I had accomplished enough,
become whatever inchoate thing I once aspired to be,
then heard as surely as if spoken to, Do the work, the
rest will follow.

How the end and beginning of stories are always lies
because both deny the thousand-stranded skein
that always ends later
and begins before

but how even this cannot divert a heart from a journey
or a poem until at last, as Rodin said of any art,
each must be abandoned but
is never finished.

No Free Verse

On Arriving in Nauplion Not Knowing How to Spend the Day

Would it be better to sit
in Syntagma all day,
pen poised to play,
books stacked at hand?

Or better to follow the organized plan
board the bus see the sites
do what is right
if not what I choose?

What I choose to pursue
is the gleam in my eye
the dream on the fly
a story to spin.

But I can only write out of where I've been.
Each word bears the cost
of another one lost.
For every line my words cause to grow

there's another missed where I did not go.
One poem lays waste to another:
while writing one, one loses the other.
There is a price to a poem.

St. Gregory's Hole
Aghia Sophia, Istanbul

A marble column soars, improbably pierced
by a thumb-size hole, stamen of a penumbral
floret twice the radius of a human hand.

A wish comes true, they say, if with the thumb
as center-pin one can inscribe a full circuit
on the stone with fingers spreading like a clock.

She stood aloof with condescending smile
as eager applicants strained in queue
to gain their wishes through their thumbs

Until with a start she saw that she too is a column
smudged by many years of learning
how much harder than wishing choosing is.

Janissary / Harem
Topkapi Palace

It is permitted to convert
a child, said the guide.
An adult must agree.

The female daughter,
the one over whom hangs
beauty or a parent's greed,
is sold to the harem,
abased for one fleet lust
like daughters still
until the caged bird sings
or the caged bird dies.

Her ten-year-old brother
joins the janissaries
or the gang or platoon
where all one has to take
or give is one's life.
Is he any freer than the girl-child
confined in rooms built so
doors and windows face only in?

How fragile the chance
for any male child or girl
to grow free and strong
into that good thing:

An adult who can choose to agree.

Tethered

in the Sahara

Donkeys in the desert inch forward
like lumpish slugs or aged crones,
forefeet hobbled by rags.

A milk cow, ribbed and scrawny-haunched,
seeks scant graze along the
radius of her rope.

One misstep and each could die. And I?
Bound close as heart to heart
to my certain ones,

tethered by varying lengths of loyalty
to friends and loves and place
and work and cause,

I gaze out from the ends of all my ropes
toward glistening distances
quick as a fennec,

gliding as gulls savoring their fill,
but freer than either because
of something I know.

Formation

The apparitions rise in clumps
along the horizon,
begin inching forward,
form into ranks like geese,
scatter rapidly,
reverse, gather again,
and finally glide to a landing
where she waits.

They disappear from sight.
Soon they are as busy
in her brain as Pompeiian cupids
focused on their appointed tasks.

She waits intently,
lends a hand where she can.
In time, astounded, she watches them
stride in contented cadence
down her arm to take
their necessary places
precisely on the page.

Second Harvest

No one follows where machines
reap wheat. Their sweep is clean.
But where terrain or need
require the scythe,
two harvests happen.

Owners send their minions
through the fields
to load their caravans
for the port before hurrying
to the adjoining field
to reap its profit too.

Evening creeps,
and second harvesters arrive,
women gleaning what others
left behind upon the ground
or close against high weeds.

One knows the need
of more than food.
Her staple crop is stories.
She works in stealth,
taking only leavings
no one else would see
or need or claim to own.

These she will glean,
grind, mix, knead,
let rise with the yeast of words.
These loaves distributed,
her granary is restored.

Revised

The lapping waters laughed
when the traveler returned home at last
from gleaming Asia to gentle Sirmio.

But it was not the same Catullus
who came home to those familiar shores
and longed-for kiss of sheets—

says one who wrestles upon return
with how to take up the threads of life
and loom she left so long ago behind.

From distant shores she brings back eyes
refracting an iridescence brighter
than the light she left.

The designs and dyes are different now,
the tension tauter on warp and woof
from all she saw in Marrakesh.

Penelope Returning

Alone on the shore of Ithaca, Penelope sat
absorbed in the shimmer of the dusk-bronzed sea,
searching for ways to tell what happened
after Odysseus came home at last.

Once he had powered his way into
his rightful place with his great bow,
she loosed the string of hers,
her vigil done, her only child now launched

beyond the reach of his mother's kind eyes
hiding the worries that circled her counsel
throughout his life, the two decades she
leaned toward him with all her weight and wit.

She conceived her plan a year after Odysseus's return,
waited patiently until the time was right.
Mentes arrived to rest his merchant crew,
take provisions, visit Ithaca for the night.

In early morning upon their olive bed
she turned quietly to Odysseus and said:
"I'll go to Egypt now. I've always wanted to.
Mentes will take me. I'll be safe, I know."

Her husband swung his gaze toward her,
mind churning with all the habits of manhood
the world and his birth had prescribed,
once again caught by the force of her courage.

Odysseus had loved her first for her beauty,
hard thereafter for her far-arching heart,
soon upon that for her lively competence,
the gift that promises a partnership for life.

"Yes," he nodded, "of course." He knew his wife.
In the day she gathered what she needed
for the journey, then put half of it away.
Half her joy the thought of traveling light.

She prepared a feast for the evening meal,
embraced the household, turned with a heavy heart
and lightness of step to board the craft
that would give to her the world.

As they rounded the western shoals
of Cephalonia she began to comprehend
what she had done. Demons of doubt
raised their frenzied whirl around her.

Guilt eroded her resolve as she wept
inconsolably, salt tears mixed with spray
at the stern where she fixed her eyes back
toward the home she left with such apparent ease.

She cried without trying to stop, only later
identifying guilt as the first monster
she must face and overcome. Others loomed
as soon as she pondered all she left behind:

How would father and son get along in her absence,
still new to each other and so little together,
son learning to become a man at the same time
Odysseus at last was learning to father?

Would they eat meals at tables
laced with thought and conversation,
or merely feed their hunger grazing
as they passed the cooking fires?

A serving girl, Melantho's daughter,
shifty-eyed and waitful, watched her depart;
Penelope saw her calculating her chances
with the master while the mistress was away.

Then, as the ship split the gentling waves
into the open sea, a moment came, still
as a hummingbird suspended, when she felt
duty fade and the joy of solitude encircle her

like the lifting light shining around
a well-loved child in love with life,
but burnished now far brighter by all
she knew from all the living she had earned.

Turning confident toward the bow, she did not
again look back. She reached Egypt,
climbed the pyramids as she had dreamed,
ate alone at dusk, made strange new friends.

No suitors waited slaying on her arrival home,
for she had razed hers one by one upon the road.
Like a sphinx, she left their leers in the markets
leveled with lances from her steely gaze.

With one like-minded journeyer she shared a meal;
Every story sparked another, flint for one another's steel.
They parted with regret, braced only by guessing
how great the love at home that taught each how to love.

Still he is lodged in her heart's estate
that no heir will ever know,
nor gaggle of glaring shrews who confuse
their envy with their rectitude.

She is home. To most she seems the same,
though the sun's magic has settled on her skin,
her hair gleams free as a dancing child's,
turquoise eyes ashine with something new.

For a while she is strangely lonely,
chooses selectively the duties she resumes,
finds it hard to become host of her own home again
after being so long a guest of the world.

She delights to give the gleaming gifts
chosen so carefully for her beloveds,
sorrowing only that she must meter the density
of detail of how she came upon each prize.

She rises, returns to the hearth of her heart's desire,
knows at last that Ithaca is not the journey
but the sharing of the stories
that make the journey known.

Acknowledgements

Any writer yearns for an appreciative reader. I am forever grateful to my first one, my second-grade teacher Thelma Lofland, who wrote in a note to my mother:

> One morning as Susan skipped to school, she made up a little poem which was all her own. Upon entering the classroom, she sat down and put her poem on paper. Then she wanted me to read it. I did, and I was amazed that a little second-grader could put into writing so well her thoughts.

Decades later I attended two poetry workshops of A.E. Stallings on the Greek island of Spetses. Among the many things I learned from Alicia are that sometimes a title can do part of the work of a poem--and that my poem "You Can't Marry Everyone You Love" is, to my surprise, a sonnet.

My friendship with classicist Nancy Felson, author of *Regarding Penelope*, began in graduate school in a seminar on Homer's *Odyssey*. She and I have shared many of life's journeys.

I am honored that Laura Hill of Cordelia Hollis approached me about publishing this book. She is one of the best book people I know.

www.ingramcontent.com/pod-product-compliance
Lightning Source LLC
Chambersburg PA
CBHW022021290426
44109CB00015B/1257